easy st

to healing

Penguin Books Australia Ltd
487 Maroondah Highway, PO Box 257
Ringwood, Victoria 3134, Australia
Penguin Books Ltd
Harmondsworth, Middlesex, England
Penguin Putnam Inc.
375 Hudson Street, New York, New York 10014, USA
Penguin Books Canada Limited
10 Alcorn Avenue, Toronto, Ontario, Canada M4V 3B2
Penguin Books (N.Z.) Ltd
Cnr Rosedale and Airborne Roads, Albany, Auckland, New Zealand
Penguin Books (South Africa) (Pty) Ltd
5 Watkins Street, Denver Ext 4, 2094, South Africa
Penguin Books India (P) Ltd
11, Community Centre, Panchsheel Park, New Delhi 110 017, India

First published by Penguin Books Australia Ltd 2000

10 9 8 7 6 5 4 3 2 1

Design by Erika Budiman, Penguin Design Studio
Cover photography by Tat-Ming Yu
Typeset in 9.75/16 pt New Baskerville by Post Pre-press Group, Brisbane
Printed in Australia by Australian Print Group, Maryborough

National Library of Australia
Cataloguing-in-Publication data:

Allica, Greer, 1944– .
  Easy steps to healing : repairing body and soul.

  ISBN 0 14 029315 9.

  1. Self-help techniques. 2. Healing. 3. Mental healing. I. Title.

158.1

www.penguin.com.au

I dedicate this book to my daughter, Mirren,
who has been my unfailing friend on our journey
together. Like me, she dared to believe that a
dream could come true.

Dear Reader,

TRANSFORMATION is in every act, every thought, every feeling. Just as every cell in your body continually renews itself, so do you continually evolve as a person.

When you are hurt, depressed or unhappy, it is likely that you are trapped by self-destructive thoughts. You think that no one understands you, that nothing can shift your problem, and that something – or someone – must bring about change. You forget that change and renewal are actually within you.

Before you can run you must learn to walk. If you can begin to see *one* ray of light where before you saw only darkness, you have taken your first step to healing. You

don't need a grand or far-reaching plan –
just small practical steps, small changes in
attitude. Sometimes the simplest solutions
are the most effective because they are the
most accessible.

Healing can only take place when you
first seek to understand yourself. Have
courage and believe that you *can* do
something about your problem when you
stop making it insurmountable or someone
else's responsibility. Take this step and have
faith that then you will receive the help and
support you need.

Miracles begin in small ways. Take the
first step and the rest will unfold.

GREER ALLICA

Gaze at a star-lit sky

A STAR-STUDDED SKY is a magical sight.
Light emerges from darkness, yet without
the darkness the star is indistinguishable.
A star-lit sky symbolises possibilities.
Its vastness puts your own life, your
own problems, into perspective.
Its beauty inspires.

Surrender

IT'S A BEAUTIFUL WORD. It means give in,
not give up. Stop struggling. Stop fighting.
Accept that the situation you face *at the
moment* is beyond your ability to handle. Why
think that you have to cope on your own?
Why think that you are deficient if you don't
have all the answers now?

Watch trees on a windy day

SMALLER BRANCHES BEND AND TWIST, moving in the direction the wind wants to take them. The trunk of the tree stands firm and allows the wind to slide around and past it. There is a dance between the wind and the tree. They know the part each must play and the pattern of their union. There is no fighting, no resistance.

Move on, move on

YOU ARE A TRAVELLER OF LIFE. Along the
road there are detours that force you to take
another direction. There are small bumps
and huge hurdles. As you come to the
detours, bumps and hurdles, remind
yourself to look beyond them. Move on,
move on. Don't become paralysed by the
'difficulty' you see before you.

Visit a beach at dusk

DUSK CLOSES THE DAY. It's a gentle passing, an adjustment from light to dark. Nature prepares to rest and recharge. It's a settling time. Be still. Hear the sounds of the ocean, wave upon wave. Everything passes.

Centre yourself

CONFLICT BETWEEN TWO PEOPLE sets up jagged energy waves that only multiply. Disengage yourself from the people around you. Still your thoughts. You don't need to justify your feelings or words. Nor do you need to set the other person right. You can't *make* someone understand your position. Fruitful engagement can only come when both people are receptive.

Commune with nature

ALL LIFE HAS ENERGY. Discover the uplifting and healing power of nature; discover its special energy. Feel the sacredness of the earth and respect it as you would a loved one. Go into the bush and listen to the sounds of nature. Hear the rustle of wind in the trees, the creaking and sighing of branches; watch the ants and the insects.

Write a new script

YOUR MIND HAS A SCRIPT for living. Every day you follow the words of your script, whether you're aware of it or not. You think things happen to you, but in reality it is *you* who make things happen, according to your script. Take time to listen to the thought patterns you live by and rewrite the scripts that no longer benefit you.

Read about the lives of others

READING TAKES YOU OUTSIDE of yourself. It broadens your world and opens you to new experiences and situations. Biographies – books about the lives of others – are a good start because they give examples of mentors and role models. Mentors provide the sound advice you need to find your own direction on your particular life path. Role models show you how to do something better or differently.

Program success

DO YOU HAVE UNATTAINABLE GOALS and
make impossible resolutions? Don't set
yourself up for failure. Know your
capabilities and be patient with your
progress. Plan, play and practise. Enjoy the
process, release your expectations and
success will come in its own time –
and its own way.

Watch a child play

YOU MIGHT BE TEMPTED TO JOIN IN! Have
you forgotten the simple pleasures of play?
Remind yourself. Don't think you're too
'adult' to play. Begin by building a
sandcastle. Allow yourself. Play is instinctive.
It's all about joy and laughter. You can't
worry *and* play. Nor can you play *and* remain
downhearted. Play is naturally uplifting.

Stop! Do absolutely nothing

REPLACE DOING WITH BEING. This will help
you align your thoughts and quieten your
emotions. It will arrest your mood's
downward spiral and give you the breathing
space to say to yourself: 'Now hang on,
what's going on here?' To do nothing *can*
be productive.

Focus on the main issue . . .

. . . OF WHATEVER IS WORRYING YOU. Don't get bogged down in detail or distracted by other related issues. If you do you'll become overwhelmed and give up. In order to focus you must still your mind. Breathe in and out, in and out. Focus only on the breath until you feel calm and composed.

Have a massage

IT'S THERAPEUTIC. Massage loosens and
tones the body. It improves blood circulation
and the elimination of waste. Best of all, it
relieves stress. Choose a lavender- or
chamomile-based oil for a relaxation
massage; a geranium base to release
emotions. Try rosemary or basil essences
for a deep-tissue massage.

Make a list of priorities

THESE ARE THE THINGS you *want* to do, not what others want you to do or what you feel you ought to do. Circle the three most important priorities in your life and make a poster for each. Include photos, pictures and images that illustrate and support your intentions. Put the posters in a prominent place so you'll be reminded to act.

Laugh

LAUGHTER IS A TONIC and a balm. Laughter
alters your perspective. Watch a funny
movie. Could you turn your present conflict
into a humorous situation? When you're
miserable it's difficult to see the funny side.
But what if you could? Play around with the
situation in your mind until you see
the comedy.

Think positive

AN OPTIMIST SEES THE BRIGHT SIDE of every
situation. To bridge the gap between
negative and positive sometimes seems
impossible. It's not. You just need to acquire
the skills of a mental acrobat, a juggler of
thoughts. Take note and catch the negative,
but throw the positive into view.

Buy a lottery ticket

THE JOY OF ANTICIPATING what you would
do with the winnings is well worth the price
of the ticket. By exercising your imagination
in this way you might actually get in touch
with what you *really* want to do in life.
Whether you win or not, a lottery ticket
might be the beginning of positive
changes in your life.

Remember something
you did well

YOU MAY NOT BE COPING NOW, but that's all
it is – now! It's so easy to generalise from this
thought and tell yourself that you *never* cope,
that you're hopeless and can't do anything
well. Don't become self-destructive. Make
a list of the things you *can* do. Shout them
to the world and to your denigrating
internal voice. Write them down.

Give yourself a present

THE PRESENT doesn't have to be big. It doesn't even have to cost money. But it *must* be something you'd like. Giving to yourself isn't selfish or indulgent – forget that critical self-talk. Remember that giving to anyone – including yourself – is nourishing. It fills the empty well.

Change the way you look

THE WAY YOU LOOK is a reflection of your inner self. When you change the outer self you fool the ego. By doing this you create a small crack in your emotional armour, which then enables you to begin the process of change at a deeper level. Wear a colour, style or item of clothing that you don't normally wear.

Enjoy time with a friend

WHEN YOU'RE FEELING DOWN it's easy to become trapped by negative thinking. You keep your own company because you feel that no one else could bear to be with you. Don't be so hard on yourself! Friends are there to share *every* part of you. They don't expect you to be happy all the time. By revealing your vulnerability you invite support.

Be grateful . . .

. . . FOR WHAT YOU HAVE without thinking
of what you *might* have. Be grateful for who
you are without thinking of who you *might*
be. You are unique and can't be compared.
Find the gift that you have to share.

Dance

HAVE YOU HEARD OF DANCE THERAPY? Did
you know you can dance out your emotions
and your thoughts? It's an integrating
activity, bringing all parts of your being into
play. Whether you dance for therapy or just
for the sheer joy of movement doesn't
matter. Afterwards you'll feel uplifted and
more in touch with your whole self.

Be creative

'OH NO!' you say, 'I've never painted a thing in my life.' Creativity is so much more than painting. Creativity is a necessity for life and living. It's the act of bringing anything into being through the power of your mind and imagination. Self-expression is the result of creativity.

Study the birds

A BIRD SOARS WITHOUT TRYING. To fly is
part of its genetic inheritance. Lifting off
from land's edge, a bird spreads its wings
and trusts. In a symbolic way you too can
give yourself wings. Think of a bird's
effortless flight and fly beyond the fears that
limit and ground you. Free yourself.

Indulge

HAVE A GLASS OF WINE or a piece of cake –
anything you don't normally allow yourself.
Let go of your judgemental 'parent' and
remember that it's not wrong to indulge
occasionally. *Enjoy* your indulgence!

Do something practical

YOU CAN SEE THE RESULT of a practical act.
You can't distort or magnify it as you might
do with your problems. Doing something
practical puts you in touch with the 'real
world' again by putting your ego back in its
place and allowing you to develop a
broader perspective.

Walk

WALKING IS MORE THAN A PHYSICAL ACT.
The simple, rhythmical action of placing
one foot in front of the other calms your
mind and activates both sides of the brain as
the right arm swings forward in time with
the left leg. The analytical left brain, with its
attention to detail, can now work in
combination with the intuitive right brain,
which sees the broader picture.

Breathe in light

IMAGINE YOU ARE SURROUNDED BY LIGHT.
Breathe it in through the pores of your skin
or through the crown of your head. Suffuse
your whole body with light. By doing this
you change the quality of your energy,
which then affects your mental and
emotional state.

Watch the sun rise

STAND SILENTLY AND WATCH the sun emerge
from the horizon. At first it's a pale light
that steals out of darkness, then it spreads
and multiplies. Light gathers lightness and
colour, heralding the dawn. Darkness
recedes. Light takes over and another
day begins.

Pray

IF YOU HAVE A SPIRITUAL VIEW of the world, prayer will lift you out of the depths. Have faith and surrender to a higher intelligence. The act of prayer brings a measure of peace and, eventually, answers. If you are a non-believer, imagine a group mind that is greater than your own and therefore capable of shedding light on your problems.

Give thanks

NO ONE IS AN ISLAND. We all depend on
our own support networks of friends, family,
partners and work colleagues. Give thanks to
all these important people in your life. Ring
one of them or pay them a visit.

Take up a new hobby . . .

. . . OR MAKE TIME for an existing one.
Hobbies are pastimes pursued out of love,
free from pressure and untainted by money.
They remind you about 'attitude' – it affects
every part of your life. Imagine if you
regarded your job in the same way you
regarded your hobby.

Express yourself
through painting

PLAY A PIECE OF BEAUTIFUL MUSIC and
breathe deeply for a few minutes. On a sheet
of watercolour paper that has been entirely
painted with water, drop pools of colour.
Let the colour make its own patterns and
shapes. How can you interpret them?
Look at your colour choice. What does
it symbolise?

Contact your higher self

QUIETEN YOUR MIND AND BODY by
breathing deeply. Imagine a shaft of white
light above you, then visualise a small
pinprick in the crown of your head. Draw
this light, which represents your higher self,
into your being. Hold a conversation with it.
Ask for guidance.

Be humble

IT'S PERHAPS AN OLD-FASHIONED WORD, but it's not an old-fashioned attitude. We're all guilty of playing God now and again or wanting to take centre stage. If you can put yourself back in your place and do it with humour, you are a wise person.

Bathe yourself in blue

BLUE IS THE COLOUR of universal love. It is
soothing, non-judgemental. Blue is also the
colour of the throat chakra, the spiritual
energy centre, responsible for your
personal expression. As you breathe in blue,
see yourself relating kindly and lovingly
to others.

Find compassion

COMPASSION IS AN UPLIFTING EMOTION.
It's the ability to look kindly on others
without judgement or comparison. All the
great religious teachers have taught
compassion. Compassion implies acceptance
and forgiveness and should not be confused
with pity, which is a demeaning emotion.
Be compassionate also with yourself.

Don't expect so much

WHEN YOU EXPECT A LOT from yourself and
others you make the going so hard.
Expectations are rods of your own making;
they make you judgemental and sap your
confidence. How can you live with joy when
you're weighed down by unrealistic
standards?

Exercise

EXERCISE RELEASES NORADRENALIN into the
brain cells, which makes you feel elevated
and energised. Exercise is good for toning
the body and releasing pent-up emotions
such as grief, anger and guilt. Exercise is a
prelude to meditation.

The past is over

ARE YOU LIVING YOUR PRESENT in the past?
If so, it's time to let go. Don't perpetuate the
past by continuing to nurse old hurts. The
way you live now, the thoughts you have now,
are already creating your future. If you want
a different future, be prepared to forgive –
not forget – the past.

Remove yourself . . .

. . . FROM A STRESSFUL SITUATION so that you have time to recover, evaluate and understand. Sometimes it will be impossible to physically leave a situation. At such times remove yourself mentally. Concentrate on a beautiful or secure scene or repeat an affirming thought.

Light a candle

IT'S NOT ALWAYS EASY to control your mind
and emotions. It takes years and years of
learning and understanding, so sometimes
it's necessary to do something concrete and
physical to break a negative cycle. A candle
flame is a symbol of hope. Make it your
symbol and light a candle. Use it as a trigger
to shift your mood.

Step outside

THESE TWO SIMPLE WORDS hold the key to mastering a difficult situation. 'Step outside' your subjective views. Imagine a padlocked fence or a locked door through which you must pass. Under a stone you find the key, and as you pass through your barrier notice what it is made of, what it looks and feels like. By doing this you will discover what keeps you locked in your present situation.

Drop your load

IMAGINE YOU ARE CARRYING an enormous
load on your back. Name it. Does this
burden belong to someone else? If it does,
give it back. If it doesn't, tell yourself that
you've taken on more than you can cope
with. Find a suitable place to off-load. Your
place might be a rubbish dump, a grave or
the top of a mountain.

Sing

IT DOESN'T MATTER whether you sing a song
or just intone sounds. To sing is to express.
Expression relates the inner 'you' to the
outer world. Sound is made up of vibrations,
some of them calming, unifying and
uplifting. Play with different sounds.
Make them resonate and see how they
affect your body and your mood.

Make a bridge

IN AN IMPOSSIBLE SITUATION try building a
mental bridge from where you are to where
you want to be. Your bridge tells you about
possibilities, alternatives and flexibility.
You are in charge of the construction, the
blueprint for your life. Make your blueprint
the best it can be because every thought
defines your future.

Hear the birds

HAVE YOU EVER SAT QUIETLY in a garden or in the bush and listened – really listened – to the song of birds? Let their calls resonate and fill your whole being until you are aware of nothing else but the song of birds. Find your own song, a song to rejoice and live for.

It takes two

IN ANY SITUATION OF STRESS or conflict,
remember it takes two. There are two
protagonists, two sides of an argument,
two sets of responsibilities and at least two
outcomes. Look at it this way: you have half
the load, half the answer, and you bear
responsibility for half the blame and half
the outcome. You need only take care
of *your* half!

This, too, will pass

MAKE THIS YOUR MANTRA, prayer, song or
affirmation. Repeat it, write it, pray it,
remember it, visualise it. Know that your
circumstances change, and that what is
unbearable now might be the making of you.
Bless the situation for whatever it has to
teach you about life. Learn graciously.

Be vulnerable

YOU MIGHT THINK that by being vulnerable
you allow others to hurt you, but the
opposite is true. By being vulnerable you
invite support from others; you show that
you are human, you are not perfect. You
reveal yourself so that others may better
understand and respect your whole being.

Let go of the controls

WHEN A SITUATION GETS OUT OF HAND a common response is to frantically try to control it. Control feels safe. The pitfall is that the ego is involved, which means you'll assert control at someone else's expense. The ego doesn't want to see the whole picture because it's driven by fear rather than by love. Learn to relinquish control. Instead listen and seek to understand.

Go sailing

BLOW AWAY YOUR TROUBLES – and the cobwebs! Feel the wind in your hair and on your body. Feel free. Enjoy being out in the open, facing the elements. Find the brave soul within and you'll be able to face life's trials. Courage, determination and willpower will take you a long way.

Adjust

IT DOESN'T MEAN THAT YOU, a round peg,
should try to fit into a square hole – that's
the job of a contortionist! What it does mean
is that you take a good look at both the
round peg (yourself) and the square hole
(your impossible situation). With a bit of
trimming the peg might fit quite well.
Or perhaps you'll find that the hole isn't
as square as you thought.

The Garden of Eden

THE GARDEN IS A METAPHOR for your ideal situation. Imagine it. Paint it strongly in your mind so that each step you take will be a step towards its manifestation. You won't achieve your ideal all at once, and you may alter it along the way. Don't underestimate the power of your mind to bring about physical change.

We're all human

WHEN YOU'RE IN CONFLICT with someone
and you've both dug yourselves into
intractable positions, it's useful to remember
that the person you're facing is a living,
breathing, at times fearful and insecure
human being – not a devouring monster.
Don't demonise. It makes you a victim and
it encourages fear.

Compromise

IT'S EASY TO PUT YOURSELF in an all-or-
nothing situation and in so doing find that
you're stuck and unable to move. That's the
nature of all-or-nothing responses! By taking
all you find yourself alone; by taking nothing
you find yourself deprived. Look for a way
that considers your needs and those of the
other person. If compromise is not possible,
be gracious and go your own way.

Spring-clean

SPRING-CLEANING YOUR HOUSE can give you
a wonderful, light feeling. What you do on a
physical level has meaning on a deeper level.
Your house represents yourself. Cleaning it
of cobwebs and dirt and reaching into dark,
hidden corners can be the beginning of an
inner spring-clean. Clean out your
destructive attitudes and habits.

Sleep on it!

IT'S AMAZING HOW DIFFERENT things look in
the morning. Whatever your problem, let
your subconscious work on it while you
sleep. Drink half a glass of water just as you
go to bed. Visualise the problem and ask for
solutions, then drink the remaining water.
When you wake you'll be surprised by the
direction and clarity you now have.

Feel freely

ARE YOU THE SORT OF PERSON who
rationalises everything that happens to you?
Do you intellectualise your feelings so much
that you end up not knowing what you really
feel? Allow yourself to have both positive
and negative feelings. The seat of your
feelings is in your stomach. If you find your
consciousness going straight to your head,
bring it back to your stomach. Feel your
feeling. It will then be easier to move on.

Don't be immersed

IT'S GREAT TO HAVE FEELINGS but if you're
so immersed in them that you're unaware of
anything or anyone else, your view of the
world has become totally subjective and
inaccurate. Always remember that others
have feelings too. This realisation helps you
restore your perspective.

Put your hands in the earth

BY DOING THIS you literally become
'earthed'. Gardeners will tell you of the
peace and joy they find digging amongst
living, growing things. The earth gives you a
sense of proportion; it helps you to accept
what is. Everything has a pattern, a rhythm
and a flow. Get in touch with these things.

Communicate your
boundaries

BOUNDARIES REPRESENT YOUR LIMITS. Only
you know your own limits. You have gone
beyond them when you feel pain and
distress. Know yourself – know what you
can't accept. Make your limits clear to others
so that you don't feel invaded or fearful or
abused. Communicate your boundaries
clearly and respectfully.

Make contact with a neighbour

IN OUR BUSY WORLD it's easy to forget that a person just like you is living right next door. He or she faces day-to-day struggles like you do. It's a good feeling to share something of yourself, whether it's a smile, a 'How are you?' or an invitation to a cup of tea. There's always time – if you make it.

Action, not reaction

BE AWARE OF THE DISTINCTION between action and reaction. Action is what you do and say after you have considered your own position as well as that of the other person. Reaction is an unconscious response. Much of this response belongs to the other person and/or to another matter not relevant to the present conflict. Reaction will lead you away from your real concern.

Pause

IT'S LIKE TAKING A BREATH to consider or
counting to ten when you're about to blow
up. It gives you time to change your
viewpoint, to consider alternatives, to defuse
your emotional reaction. A pause won't be
an answer, but it might avoid a disaster.

Stand under an
ancient tree

OLD TREES HAVE A WONDERFUL ENERGY that
is uplifting and life-giving. You might have
heard some people talk about hugging a
tree. Suspend your scepticism and try it.
All living things have energy: see if you
can feel the pulsing energy beneath the
bark of a tree.

Consideration

IF YOU CONSIDER OTHERS you won't abuse
or denigrate. By being considerate you invite
a similar response. If you react to others'
lack of consideration by treating them in the
same way, you are only driven by *their*
agenda. Consideration encourages you to
listen and to seek understanding.

Sunning

'SUNNING' IS THE ACTIVITY of making
sunshine! There are plenty of times in life
when the situation you face seems so black
that you can't imagine a way out. That's
when you create sunshine. Imagine yourself
bathed in sunshine, warmed and cheered by
it. See yourself smiling with the sheer
pleasure and abandonment of sunning.

Think about
forgiveness

YOU MAY NOT BE ABLE to forget past wrongs
and there's no reason why you should if they
have taught you valuable lessons. Your past has
made you who you are today, but in order to
assimilate your past with your present, you
need to forgive. Forgiveness comes from the
heart and from understanding. You cannot
have forgiveness without compassion.

Good things come in threes

THINK OF THREE GOOD THINGS to do – things that will give you pleasure and happiness, that will bring back your zest for life and your belief in others.

Then do them.

Another day

IN ORDER TO MOVE OUT of a difficult
situation, picture another day and imagine
yourself in it. This day will be an easier one,
a day of your choosing. In your mind's eye
make it as vivid as you can. Bring in happy
and comforting images from your past.
Project your future ideals into this imaginary
day. See yourself being there.

Walk barefoot

GROUND YOURSELF. Get in touch with the earth and its elements. Walk barefoot through sand or grass. Feel the grains of sand slip between your toes. Feel the damp, soft grasses slide past with each step you take.

A wondrous thing!

WONDER – the ability to be in awe – is a quality children have plenty of. It feeds their interest and joy in life. It motivates them to regard life as an adventure. If you're feeling a little jaded with your life, recapture the spirit of wonder.

Hope

HOPE EMBODIES A HEALTHY APPROACH
to life. If you have hope you can allow for
people and situations to change. You
suspend judgement and expectation. In the
midst of what feels like hopelessness you
dare to imagine an improvement. Hope is
life-giving and affirming. It lifts finality away.

Name your emotion

DISCOVER WHAT'S BEHIND your present
feeling. Draw an emotional map. Behind
anger lies hurt, behind hurt lies an
expectation, behind the expectation lies a
belief, behind the belief there is an origin.
Trace your belief back to its origin. Decide
whether you want to change your belief.
Then you can change your emotion.

Reconciliation

AFTER FORGIVENESS comes reconciliation.
Reconciliation means moving from a
position of hostility to a state of friendship
and agreement. It involves reaching out.
It brings peace and harmony. It restores
balance. Reconciliation provides a firm
foundation so you can move on from a
position of strength.

Imagine

IMAGINE IF THINGS WERE DIFFERENT . . .
Your imagination has the power to lift you
out of seemingly impossible situations.
Use it. It provides a temporary escape
from negativity. Imagination helps loosen
fixed attitudes.

Face the facts

DON'T EMBROIDER, deny, procrastinate or project. Face up to yourself; be honest and realise the part you've played in getting yourself into the difficult situation you're now in. Be brave. If you can admit your part then you can mentally throw off everything else that doesn't belong to you.

Meditate

FIND A QUIET SPACE by yourself. Sit or lie
comfortably and empty your mind of all
thoughts. Allow your thoughts to float away
like clouds in the sky. Let them go. Be aware
only of the rhythm of your breathing – in
and out, in and out. Do this for ten or
twenty minutes and you'll feel more
balanced and relaxed.

Affirm yourself

IT'S OKAY TO BE the person you are. You're
allowed to mess things up; you're allowed to
be less than perfect, to not cope. When
things aren't going well it's all too easy to
berate and belittle yourself. Don't be so
harsh. Be kind and loving. Tell yourself
that you are okay.

Take comfort

COMFORT IS whatever makes you feel more at ease. Comfort is a hot-water bottle, a bowl of soup, teddy bears, hugs and cuddles, a blanket, music, a soothing drink. You can even suck your thumb if it reassures and comforts you! At times every adult has a hurt and fearful, lost and lonely child inside.

Give yourself a
medal

YOU'VE ALREADY WON and you didn't know.
Give yourself a medal for trying, and for
coping, existing and surviving. Take the
striving and strain out of struggle. Celebrate
the fact that you're alive and unique, that
you – yes, even you! – have something
wonderful to contribute.

Gather your resources

THINK ABOUT YOUR STRENGTHS and the skills you know you possess. What mental and emotional qualities are you proud of? Start with these resources when you encounter difficulty and you'll move more easily from the 'known' through the 'unknown'.

Have a relaxing bath

INDULGE IN A HOT BATH with a few drops of
an uplifting essential oil – lemon balm, rose,
bergamot, ylang-ylang, geranium, basil,
chamomile, clary sage or patchouli. Make up
your own combinations and sprinkle the oil
under the running hot water. Lie back on
your bath pillow, shut your eyes and release
all negative thoughts. Breathe them out
through the pores of your skin.

Seek advice

THERE ARE ALWAYS OTHERS who have been
through similar situations to the one you're
in now. Perhaps they can share what they
have learnt. There are many trained
counsellors and psychologists as well as
other trustworthy people who'll give you an
objective and rational view.

It's never too late . . .

. . . TO MAKE AMENDS, to start afresh, to
finish what you've begun, to look at things
in a new light and form new understandings.
Be flexible enough to allow for change in
yourself and others, even if you can't
imagine *how* change is possible.

Pick flowers for the house

SMALL CHANGES MAKE A DIFFERENCE.
Making time for an activity such as this will
get you off life's treadmill for a short while.
Bring colour and beauty into your
surroundings. Put your heart and attention
into choosing and then arranging the
flowers. Your mood will automatically lift.

Believe the best

IN EVERYTHING THAT HAPPENS TO YOU,
in everything you do, you have two choices:
to assume the worst or to believe the best of
others. When you assume the worst, you
condemn before a 'crime' is committed.
When you assume the best, you allow the
possibility of a positive outcome.

Kindness . . .

. . . IS AN UNDERESTIMATED WORD. It means
giving someone the benefit of the doubt.
It involves trust and faith. Kindness brings
out softness and gentleness; it knocks the
hard and brittle edges off people.
It eliminates struggle.

Consult the I Ching

THE I CHING OR BOOK OF CHANGES is an
ancient Chinese text that is more than five
thousand years old. It's a book of profound
wisdom, which is as relevant to our culture
now as it was in the days of Confucius.
Dip into the I Ching in your spare moments
or when you need inspiration.

Reality is an illusion

THERE ARE WORLDS WITHIN WORLDS.
You probably only know one of them.
What you think you see and know is only
part of what there *is* to be seen and known.
When you can see and hear only a part of
the truth, the reality of any situation is
distorted. Suspend your judgement and
open yourself to the broader picture.

Intuition

YOUR SIXTH SENSE or intuition is your gut
feeling about a situation or person.
Everyone has an intuitive sense, no matter
how underdeveloped. You can't pin down
intuition. If you want to access your intuition
you'll need to look beyond a scientific or
rational explanation. Use your intuition to
bypass your ego's demands and to reach an
understanding of the whole picture.

Climb a mountain

MOUNTAINS ARE CHALLENGES. Visualise or climb a mountain. From the top you can see all that you've achieved. If there were nothing left to strive for in life, you'd give up. If you want your future to be different, you'll need to look forward to the next mountain. Begin with one small step and the rest will follow.

Don't be daunted . . .

. . . BY THE ENORMITY OF YOUR TASK or by
the overwhelming hurdles you face. You can
be absolutely certain of one thing: nothing
stays the same and what was once a
mountain in time becomes a small hill and
then a flat plain. Perspectives change – even
from one day to the next!

Plan a holiday

PLANNING A HOLIDAY gives you permission
to enjoy yourself, to take time off, to stop
putting pressure and making demands on
yourself. A holiday is a reprieve – it gives you
something to look forward to. The very act
of planning it makes you feel light and
carefree. You're looking after yourself,
nourishing *all* areas of your life.

Empower yourself

BEGIN BY LISTENING TO YOURSELF. What's
the most disempowering thought you hold
in your mind? Dissect it. What lies at the
heart of it? Contact the associated emotions.
You can disown this thought by
superimposing another thought. The new
thought will be positive. It will give you
energy. Think it often. Play it back to
yourself again and again.

Take responsibility

TO MANY PEOPLE responsibility is irksome.
It's a 'should' word. Think of it this way:
response-ability is the ability to respond
rather than react. By responding and not
reacting you own what is yours. You give
yourself permission to do something about
an unsatisfactory situation and in so doing
you go from being a victim to being a person
in charge of your own destiny.

Avoid collisions

IF YOU GO HEADLONG into battle the
chances are you'll be injured. Find a way of
operating that isn't confronting or
threatening. Treat other people as human
beings and try to dissociate your feelings
about what they've said or done from a
judgement about who they are.

Saying sorry . . .

. . . IS AN ACT OF GRACE, not of capitulation.
It shows you have the humility to admit you
were wrong or insensitive or lacking in
understanding. The act of saying sorry also
gives other people a chance to back down
from otherwise irreconcilable positions.

Nothing is set in concrete

DO YOU MAKE RESOLUTION MORE DIFFICULT by looking at the damage after the event and saying: 'There's nothing that can be done now'? No matter what has been done or said in the past, you can always change your attitude towards it. It's never too late to make amends. Remember, what is now your present will soon become your past.

Put on your sunglasses!

IT'S OFTEN THE CASE that just when you need to lift your mood you're too entrenched to find a way out. That's when you put on your sunglasses with the pink, rosy lenses. Go on – it requires more imagination than effort. Now look at your situation again. Notice how everything is suffused with warmth and brightness.

Plant a seed

A SEED IS A SIGN OF PROMISE, birth and
beginning. In the heart of a seed is its
harvest. Whether you actually plant the seed
of a beautiful flower or use a seed as a
symbol is up to you. 'Bija' is the Sanskrit
word for seed. Make the bija your thought
seed, your tool for change. Plant your seed,
water it well, nourish it. Give it all the
attention it needs.

Eat carbohydrates

DID YOU KNOW that eating foods high in
carbohydrates such as bread and pasta
increases the serotonin in the brain?
Serotonin is a chemical that not only helps
induce sleep but also wards off depression.
Make sure carbohydrate-rich foods are part
of your diet.

Attract good things to your life

Do you hold deep-seated beliefs that prevent good things happening to you? Do you think you don't deserve happiness? Do you believe happiness only comes to others? Do you really *desire* it? Define what happiness means to you. Imagine good things coming into your life now.

Protection

YOUR BEST PROTECTION from pain and hurt
is to be honest with yourself and with others.
You can be honest without being brutally
honest – there are many ways to speak the
truth. You deceive yourself when you lie in
order to protect others from hurt. It's more
likely you're protecting yourself from
confronting something you'd rather
not face.

The heart centre

WHEREVER YOUR EMOTIONS HAVE LED YOU,
always bring your focus back to your heart,
the centre of love. Meditate on your heart.
Feel its beat. Breathe into and out from it
and mentally repeat the word 'love'. As you
breathe your mantra feel the essence of love,
of giving lovingly and receiving lovingly.

Do something romantic

ROMANCE BEGINS IN THE MIND. Let your imagination run wild. Do something out of the ordinary. Your romantic interlude could be big and bold – a chicken-and-champagne breakfast for two in a hot-air balloon. Or it could involve attention to detail such as leaving a note of appreciation for your loved one.

Yes you can, no you can't

DO YOU BATTLE WITH YOURSELF over the
things you can't do? 'Can't' is often based on
fear and guilt. 'Can' is empowering and
opens your mind to possibilities. 'Can'
requires courage. You have the ability.
Be affirming and assertive and say:
'I can, I can, I can!'

Wisdom grows from experience

WHEN YOU'RE IN A TROUGH and can't find a
way out, remember that it's usually not until
you're pushed that you learn. You have the
opportunity to grow from a painful
experience, so don't deny or reject new
experiences. Let them bring you wisdom,
and make your life easier.

Give up on wallowing

IT'S UNPRODUCTIVE TO WALLOW in painful experiences. Wallowing is a negative way of giving attention to yourself when you're down. Wallowing will only *keep* you down. Give yourself attention in a more positive way through a compliment or an indulgence.

Conserve your energy

WHEN YOU'RE DEPRESSED you have no
energy, you have no reserves. It's important,
then, not to overload yourself. Make sure
that you don't take on too much physically,
that you get enough sleep, that you don't
take on other people's emotional baggage.

Choose your company

SURROUND YOURSELF with positive,
life-affirming friends who'll lift you out
of your trough of depression. They are
the people who will help you – to move on,
to see another side, to reflect on what
has passed. Don't let others pull you
down further.

There's no comparison

IT'S UNPRODUCTIVE TO COMPARE your situation with someone else's or to compare yourself with another person. If you do this you make yourself envious or a victim. In either case you suffer unnecessarily. No situation is ever the same as your own, even if it appears to be so. And no person is like you. You are uniquely beautiful. Love yourself for who you are.

Have a facial

WE TALK ABOUT FACING issues and people,
about saving face, facing up to things,
making a face, putting on a face, showing
one's face and coming face to face with a
fear or a reality. Through your face you
explore the world with your senses. You
reveal yourself. Your face represents your
self-image. Let your face be pampered.

Respect

WITHOUT RESPECT FOR YOURSELF you ride roughshod over your feelings and neglect your basic needs. You are dishonest with yourself. Without respect for others you become insensitive to their differences, to their right to believe and act differently from you.

Take a risk

DO SOMETHING YOU'VE NEVER DONE before.
Say what you've never dared to say. Taking a
risk encourages you to become more
flexible. Each time you take a risk you
rehearse a feeling of fearlessness that
becomes stronger each time it is felt.
Surrender the known to the unknown.

Doodle

TAKE A PEN or a pencil and see what it does
on a piece of paper. A good doodle is
therapeutic. It releases suppressed emotions
and frustration. It's calming and absorbing
and more interesting than counting to ten!
Doodling is creative, meditative. It puts you
in touch with your non-judgemental,
non-analytical right brain.

Get rid of 'should'

'SHOULD' IS A DUTY WORD, a heavy,
suffering word. It brings guilt and
resentment, both negative emotions that
will drag you down. Every time you think:
'I should', evaluate your options. If you
really don't want to do something say: 'No'.
If you decide to do it, then feel only love,
anticipation and excitement.

Blowing bubbles . . .

. . . IS FUN. Dip a thin straw into warm soapy water. As you blow each bubble give it a name. The name represents what you wish to release. Watch the bubble pop and mentally repeat: 'I release [name]. I am now free to move on'. Breathe out and blow your next bubble.

Clues

WE LEAVE CLUES to our patterns of
behaviour lying around everywhere. Look
first at the 'faults' in others that particularly
annoy or enrage you. These, believe it or
not, are clues to a part of your personality
you haven't yet owned. Be humble enough
to take another look at yourself – in private.

Change your mind

THE SIMPLEST WAY TO SOLVE A PROBLEM
may be to change your mind about it. What
prevents you from changing your mind? It's
often pride and ego and a sense of false
loyalty or honour about the position you've
taken. Don't take yourself so seriously. Give
yourself *permission* to change your mind.

Listen

DO YOU HEAR what your 'opponent' has to
say or are you concerned with your next
sentence? If the latter is the case, you won't
move from your belief in the rightness of
your position. Because you don't listen,
you're inclined to misinterpret. If you're too
busy following the line of your own
argument you've lost you way. It won't
advance you. It will only entrench you.
Listen and learn.

Language is important

IF YOU CAN ALWAYS SPEAK in 'I', 'me' and 'my' terms when in a painful situation, you'll avoid blame and abuse. By not antagonising the other person, you'll be able to prolong the communication. If you use 'I', 'me' and 'my' you'll get in touch with what you really think and feel. You'll give the other person a chance to understand where you're coming from.

'I'm sorry'

THINK CAREFULLY. Are you the type of person who finds it difficult to apologise because you don't want to lose face? Or do you say: 'I'm sorry' out of fear or a sense of over-responsibility? An apology can work wonders, but only if you really mean it and only if you're not secretly resentful or also demanding an apology from the other person. It's no good having a qualified apology either ('I'm sorry but you . . . ').

Count

THE SIMPLE ACT OF COUNTING from one to ten and over again will bring you from boiling point to just simmering. Now instead of having to clean up the mess you've made, you have time to add the other ingredients and check the recipe. Gather your resources and view the whole picture.

Walk away

DON'T BE AFRAID TO WALK AWAY from
a confrontation. You're not a coward or
a shirker. Sometimes disengagement is
appropriate, particularly when emotions are
running high. Every situation is different.
It's helpful to tell the person before you
leave that now is not the time to discuss the
matter, that you'll talk when you've both
calmed down.

Finding your path

WHEN DISTRESSING THINGS HAPPEN it's as
though you're in a maze and can't find the
exit. Visualise this scene of many paths and
one way out. Follow each path; notice what
you see along the way. Who do you meet?
Are there any signs? As you explore and
gather information, you'll find the way out.

A mistake is a gift

DON'T BE TOO PROUD to admit when you've
been wrong. A mistake offers you an
unparalleled chance to have another go, to
reflect on what has been done and to do
things differently next time. Your challenge
is to be humble enough to *see* your mistake.
Then you can do something about it.

It could be worse

WHEN YOU'RE DOWN, try jolting yourself out
of the depths by imagining a situation worse
than your own. Visualise with all your senses.
Empathise. Return to your own situation.
Now that you've established a sense of
proportion you'll have a new outlook. You'll
see that your problem is manageable.

Work backwards

RATHER THAN PROJECTING your present
difficult situation into the future, take your
situation to its extreme and then work
backwards to the present. Look at your
particular circumstances. Ask yourself:
'What's the very worst that can happen?'
Think about what you'd do if it happened.
Then when you take yourself back to the
present it will be easier to face.

Find a trigger

FIND YOUR OWN HAPPINESS TRIGGER. It may
be the words of a song, a saying, a scene. In
order for the trigger to work you need to be
able to imagine it strongly. See it, feel it.
Practise when you don't need to use it. The
more you practise the more quickly your
trigger will activate.

Recognise your limitations

ATTEMPT ONLY WHAT IS POSSIBLE for you.
Know your own capabilities, strengths and
endurance. Don't try to do more out of guilt
or fear or comparison. No one else can
inform you about your limitations as well as
yourself. So listen without judgement.

Replace pain with
no pain

IF YOU FIND YOURSELF wanting to hurt
someone in the same way they have hurt
you, think again. Replicating pain duplicates
it. What you really seek is no pain. Stay true
to your aim. As you give love more, you'll
also receive more. Give love unconditionally
without waiting for its immediate return.

Rehearsal

WHEN A SITUATION BACKFIRES you're often
determined to act differently the next time.
But determination will desert you in the
pressure and emotion of the occasion if you
haven't done some homework. Visualise
yourself in the situation and act it out as if
you were there. Use your five senses to bring
your action alive. Practice will hasten a new
pattern and improve your chances of success.

Heroes and
heroines . . .

. . . PROVIDE MODELS OF BEHAVIOUR. They
inspire and uplift. They represent your
ideal. Find your heroes and heroines in
history or books or present-day life. Read
about them. Note what qualities you most
admire. Pin pictures of your heroes and
heroines in a prominent place. Look at
them often.

Clean out your
wardrobe

PASS YOUR OLD CLOTHES on to someone
else. Your clothes cover and protect you.
They are your interface with the world. They
represent how you see yourself and what you
show to others. By passing on your old
clothes you make a symbolic act of change.

The ripple effect

WHEN YOU THROW a pebble into water, ripples ruffle the surface. They spread out in ever-widening circles until they disappear and the water is still once more. Think of your difficult situation as that hard cold pebble. What are the ripples you've created around your pebble? Who beside yourself is affected by what you've caused? Take time to reflect on the relationship between what you do and what energy you give out to others.

Raising energy

WHEN YOU'RE DOWN, your energy becomes
scattered and depleted. Visualise a spiral of
light moving from the soles of your feet to
the top of your head. Breathe in energy.
Alternately place your hands on your solar
plexus while you breathe into and out from
it. Leave your hands there for at least
five minutes.

Be an active
participant . . .

. . . IN LIFE and you'll sail more easily
through adversity. If you're passive and wait
for things to happen to you, you're not
seizing your own freedom. You always have
a choice in every situation. You can choose
your attitude as well as your action.

Making a difference

THE ATMOSPHERE YOU GENERATE as a result
of your thoughts and your actions influences
the people around you. Think about how
you can add to the spirit of life rather than
subtract from it. You have the power to
change the world around you. Don't
underestimate or neglect this power.
Nurture it.

Write yourself a
letter of appreciation

IF YOU DON'T APPRECIATE YOURSELF and
your own capabilities you'll be easily pulled
down by other people's negative comments.
It's easy to take for granted the qualities you
have. Do you say: 'Everyone can do that,
can't they?' or 'Isn't everyone like that?'
when you receive a compliment? The next
time you receive a compliment, write it
down and stick it to a mirror or the fridge.

Aim for balance . . .

. . . BETWEEN YOUR DREAMS and the reality, between work and play, between your physical, mental and emotional selves, between your masculine and feminine sides, between the rational left brain and the intuitive right brain. Balance in all aspects of your life will bring about a greater harmony.

One step at a time

THE WAY UP FROM WAY DOWN requires you
to take one step at a time. As in the saying
'You can't run before you can walk',
remember that no one achieves miracles
overnight and that one piece of knowledge
comes on the back of another. If you're
down, make the smallest step the beginning
of your way up. Only then look for the next
step and nothing will daunt you.

Acknowledgements

To my wonderful network of family, friends and mentors – thank you for your love and inspiration.

To all those with whom I've dealt at Penguin – thank you for treating me with such genuine consideration, respect and warmth. Particular thanks to my editor, Helen Pace, for her helpful and sensitive approach.

About the author

Change and *expression* have been central
themes of Greer Allica's life . . .

A graduate of Melbourne University
with English and Political Science majors,
and a sub-major in Indian Studies, she later
studied philosophy, different religions,
psychology, mind dynamics, therapeutic
and remedial massage, yoga, reiki and
spiritual healing. Greer has been a teacher,
librarian, masseuse, counsellor, and
meditation and yoga teacher. Now, writing
and painting are her main concerns. She is
the author of *Meditation Is Easy*, which has
been translated into five languages, and
Meditation Workbook, which has successfully
sold in Australia, New Zealand, the United

Kingdom and the USA. Her paintings are represented in local galleries and private collections.